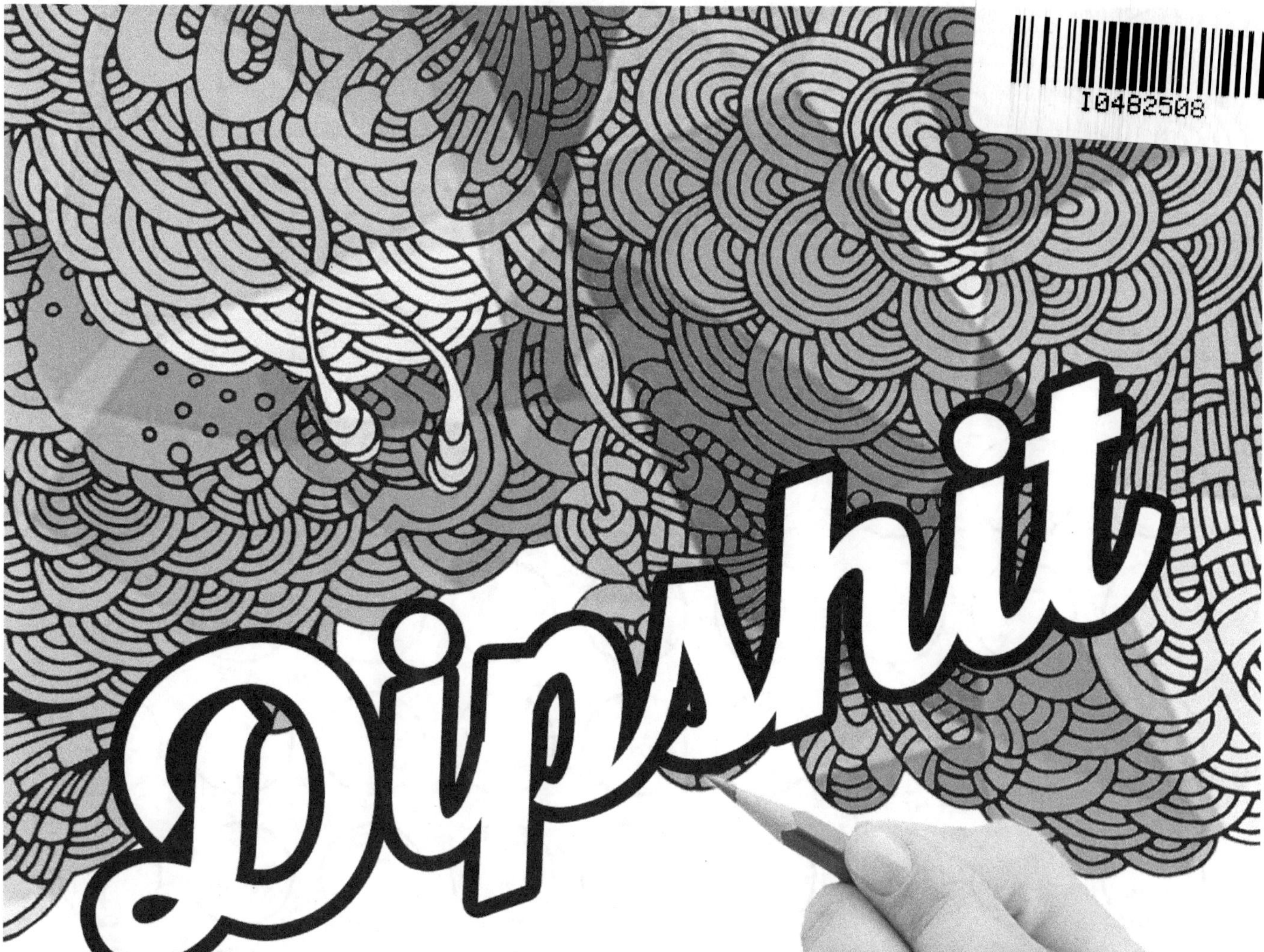

SWEAR WORD COLORING BOOK

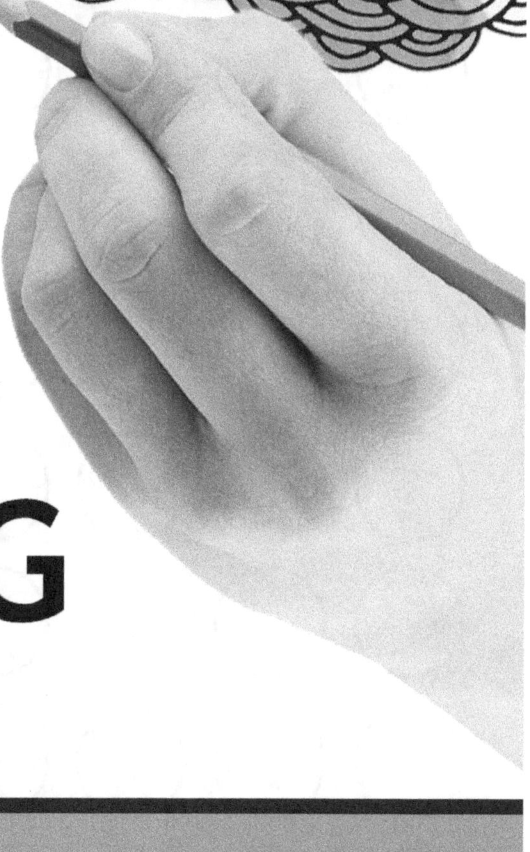

COLOR TEST PAGE

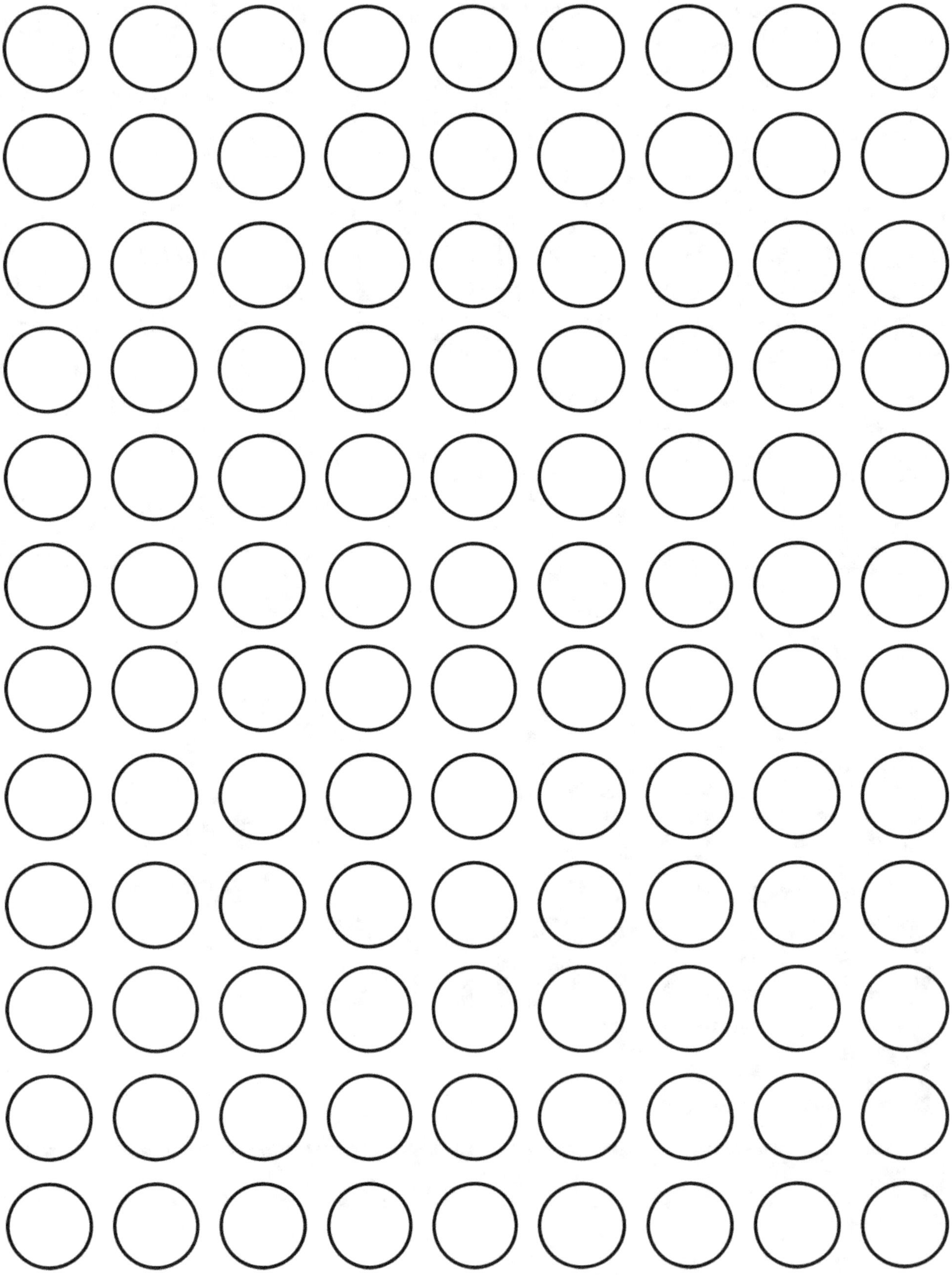

COLOR TEST PAGE

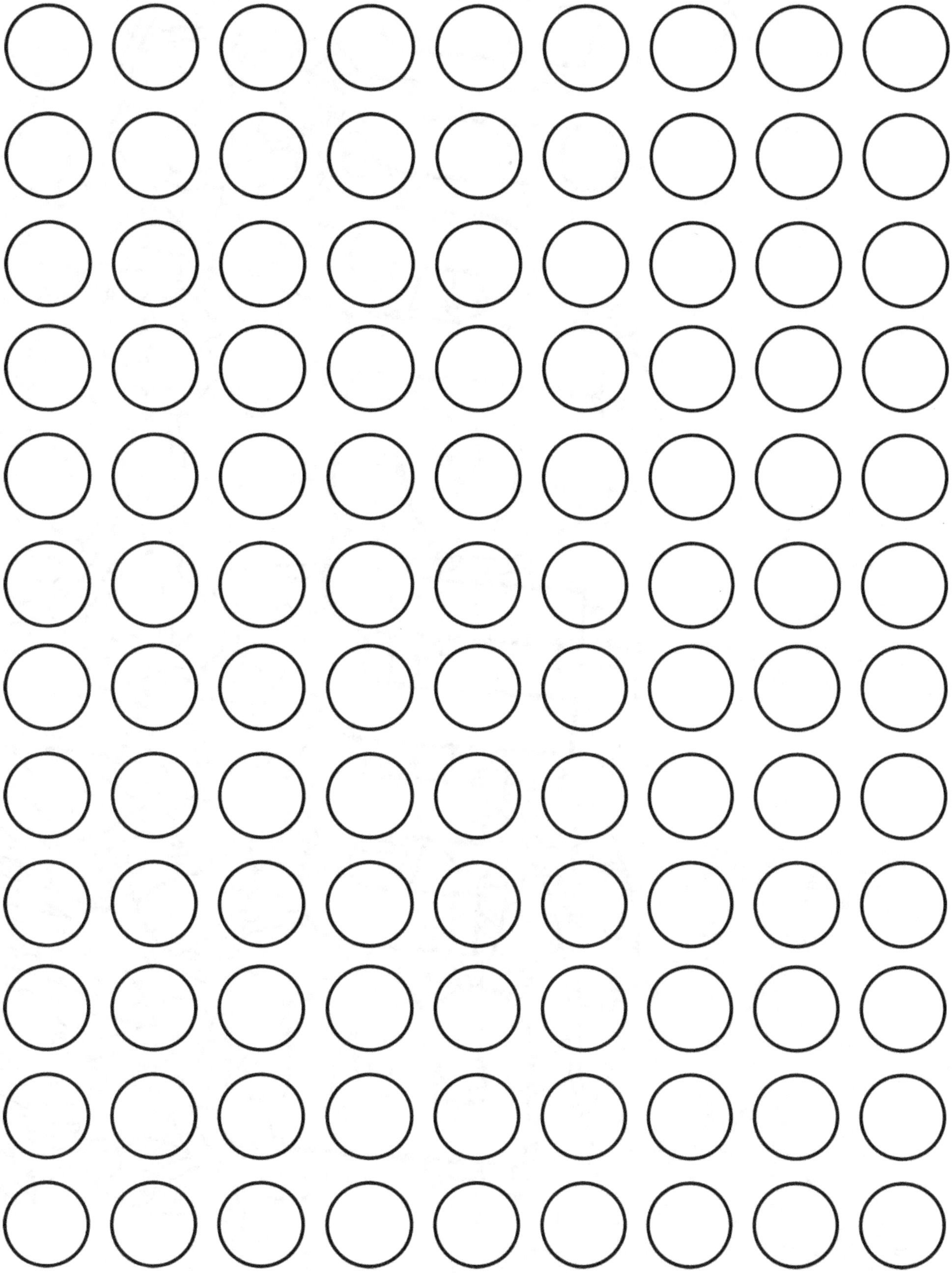

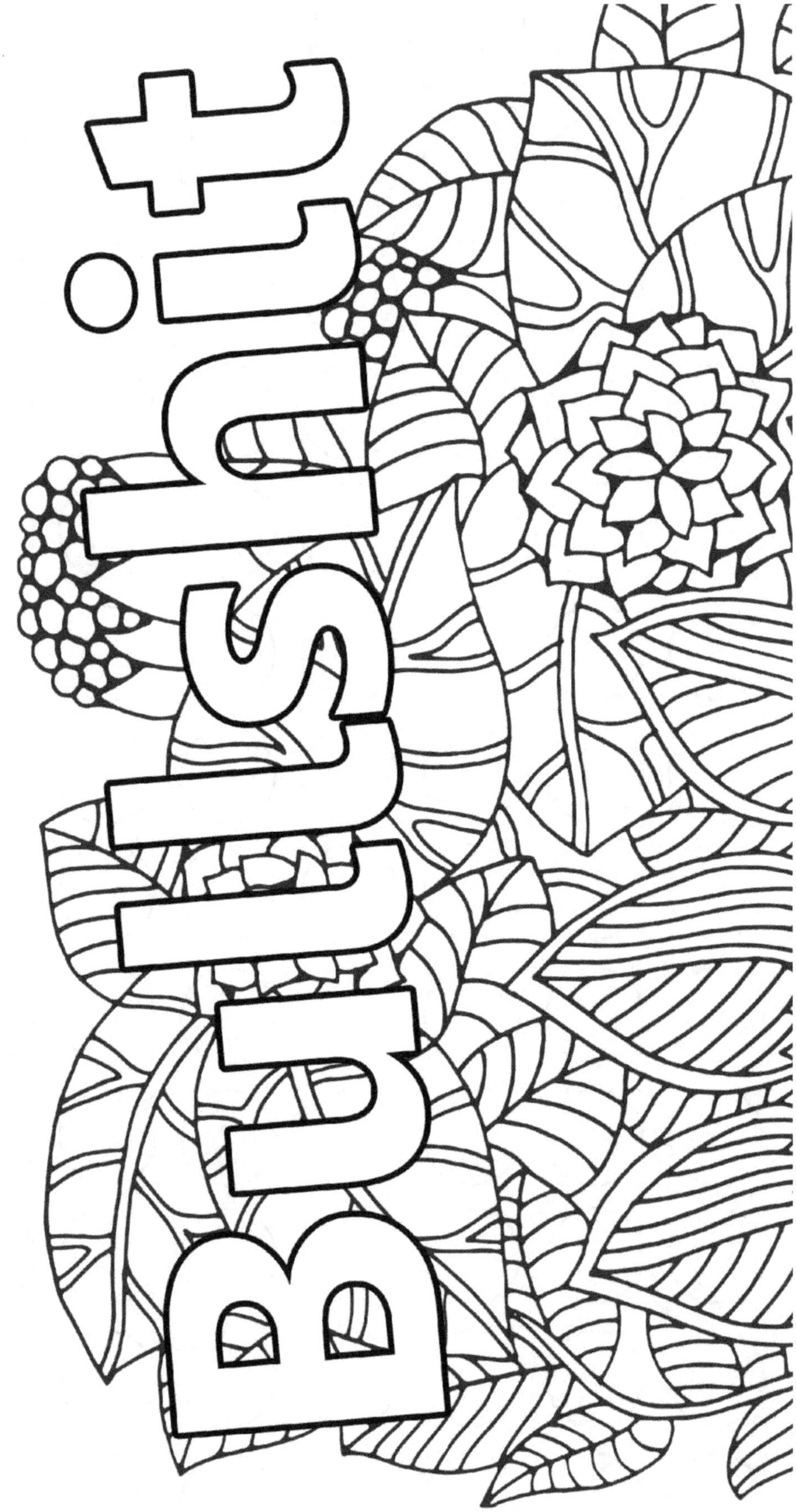
Bullshit

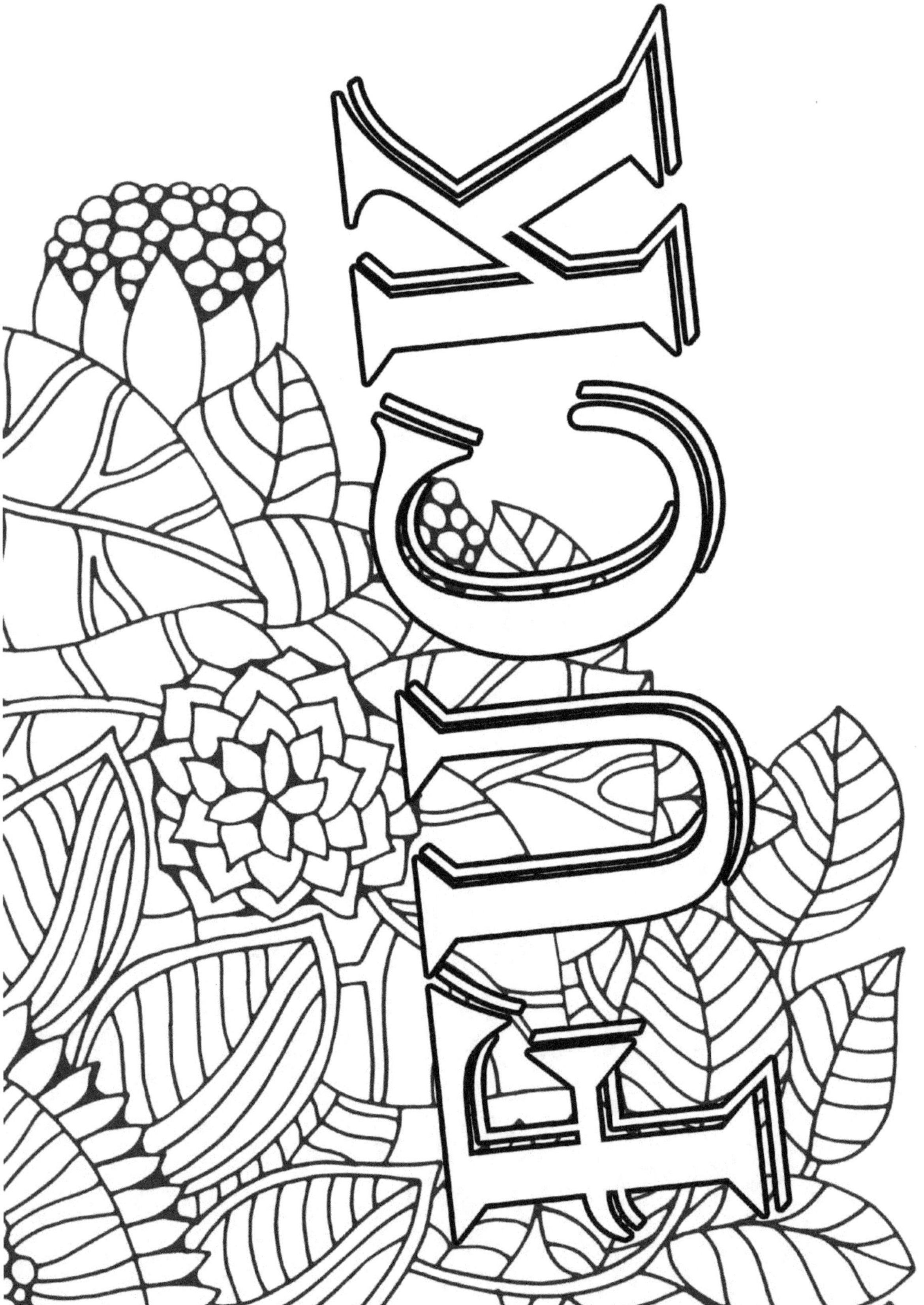
FUCK

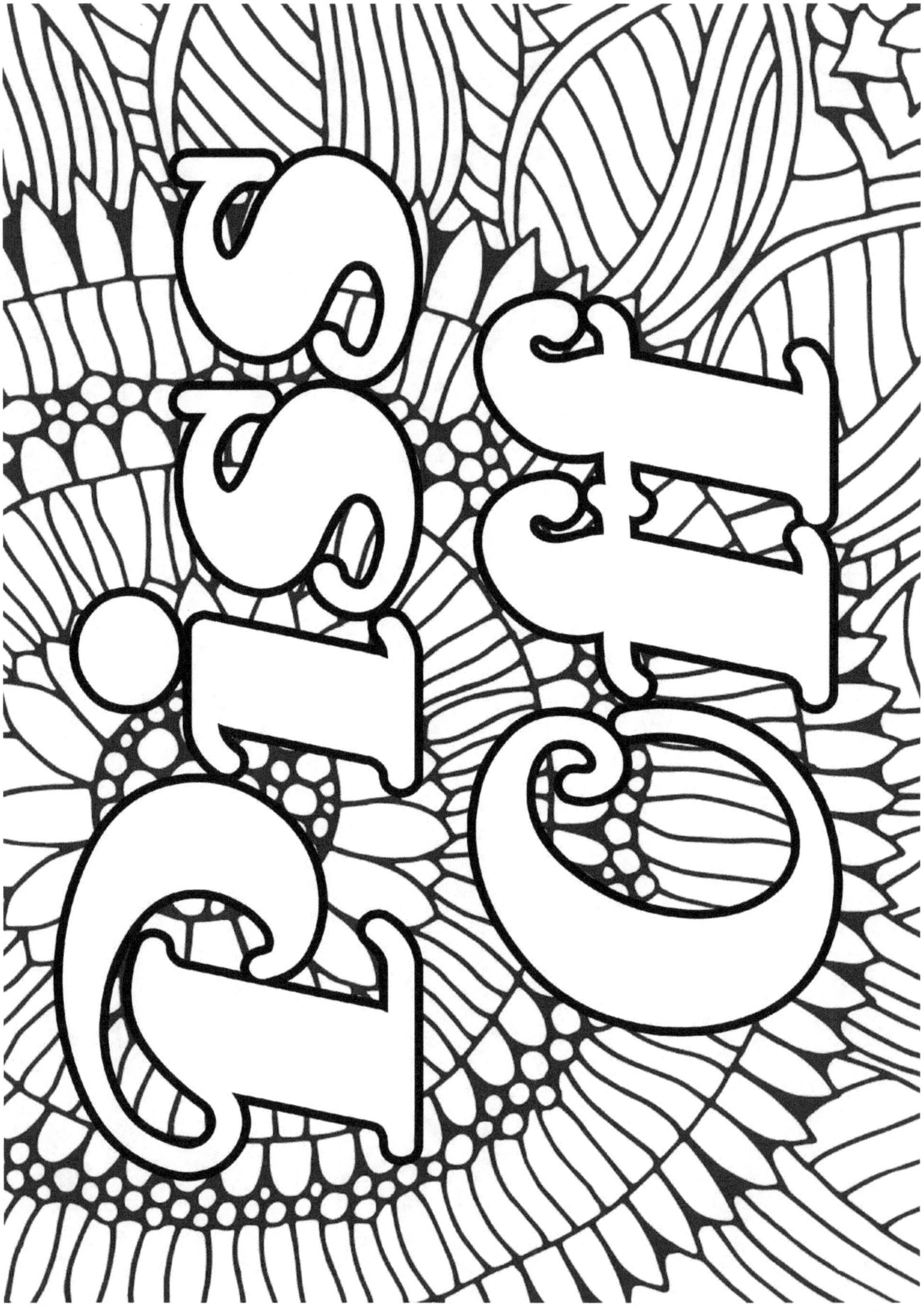
Piss
Off

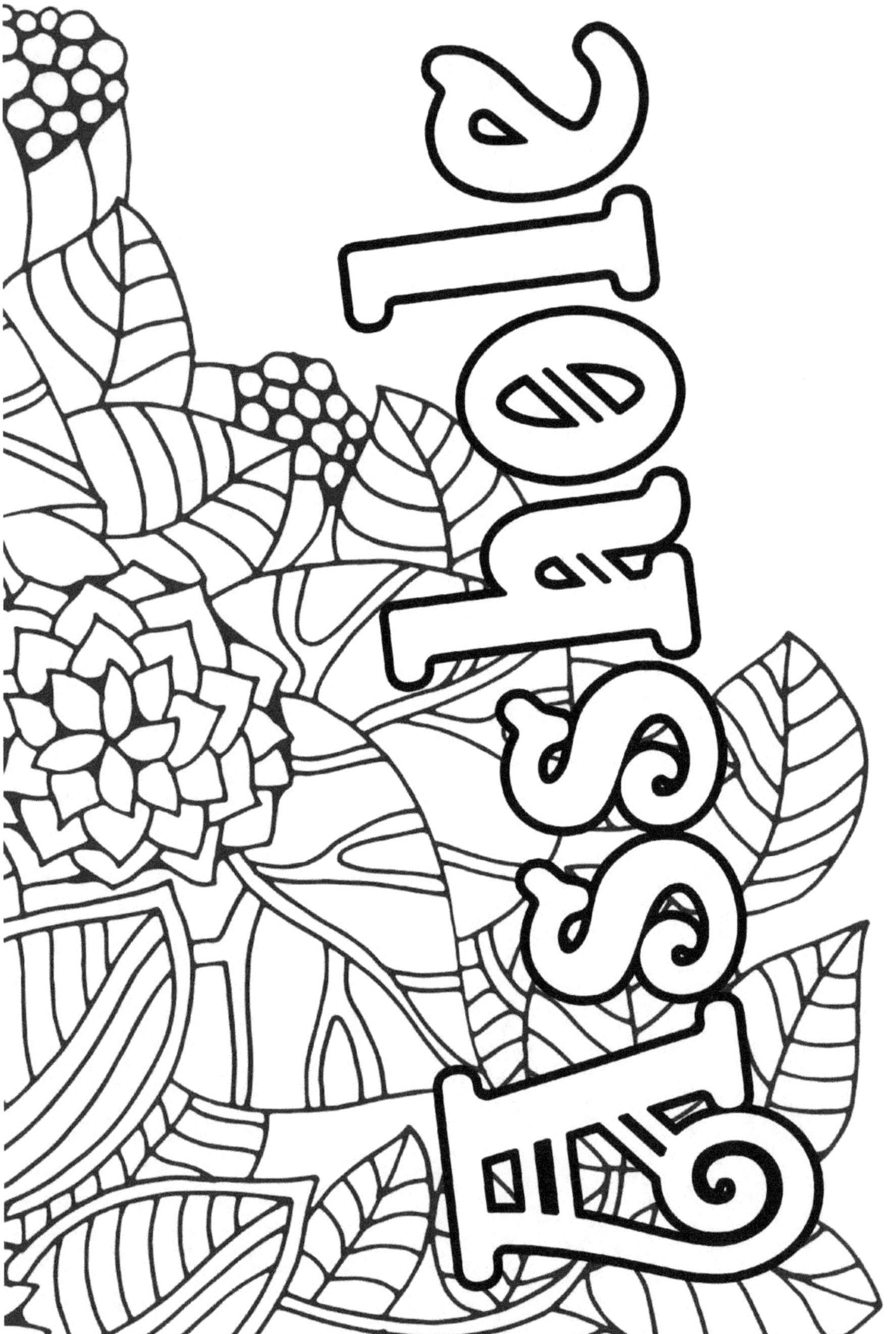
Asshole

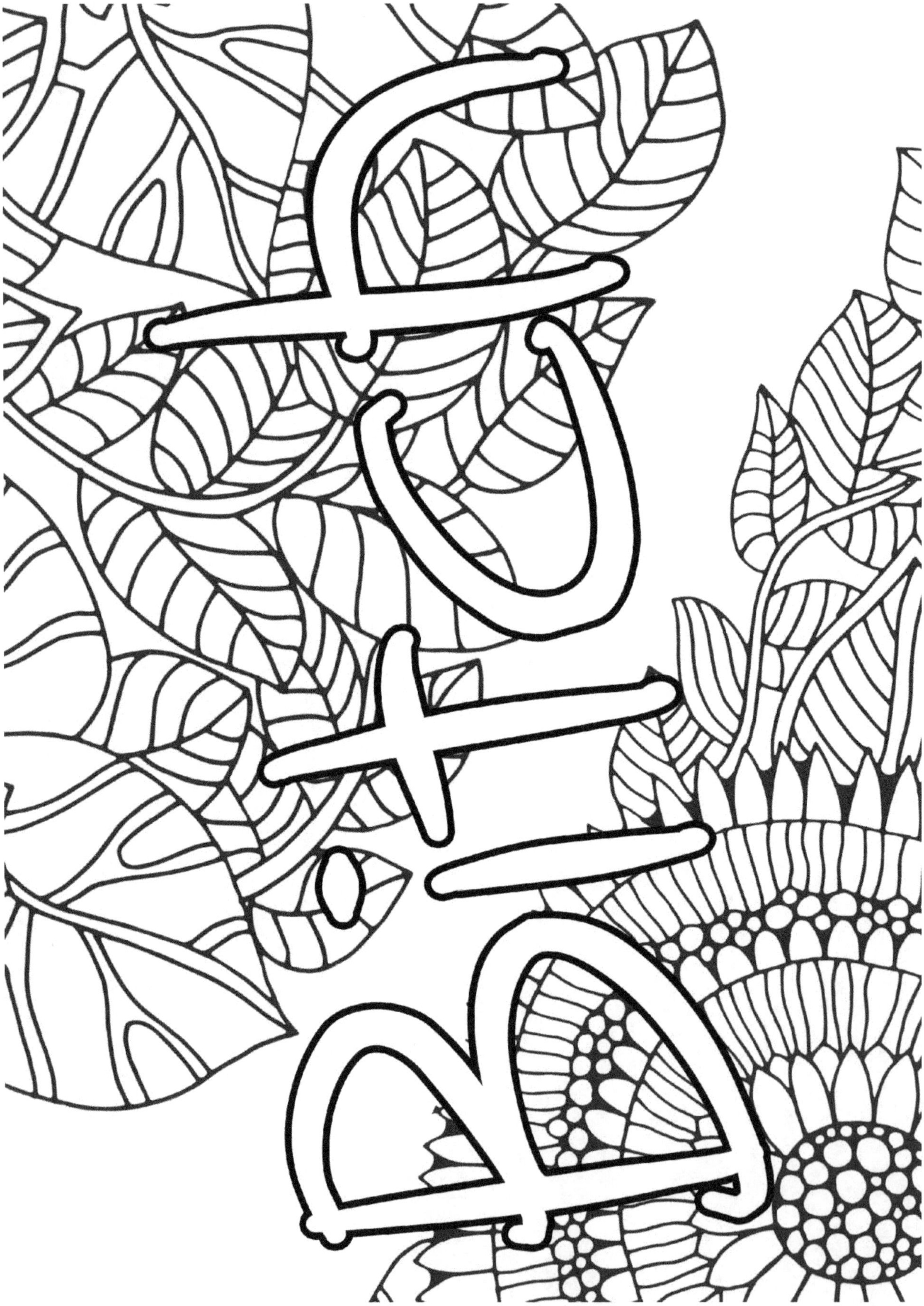
Bitch

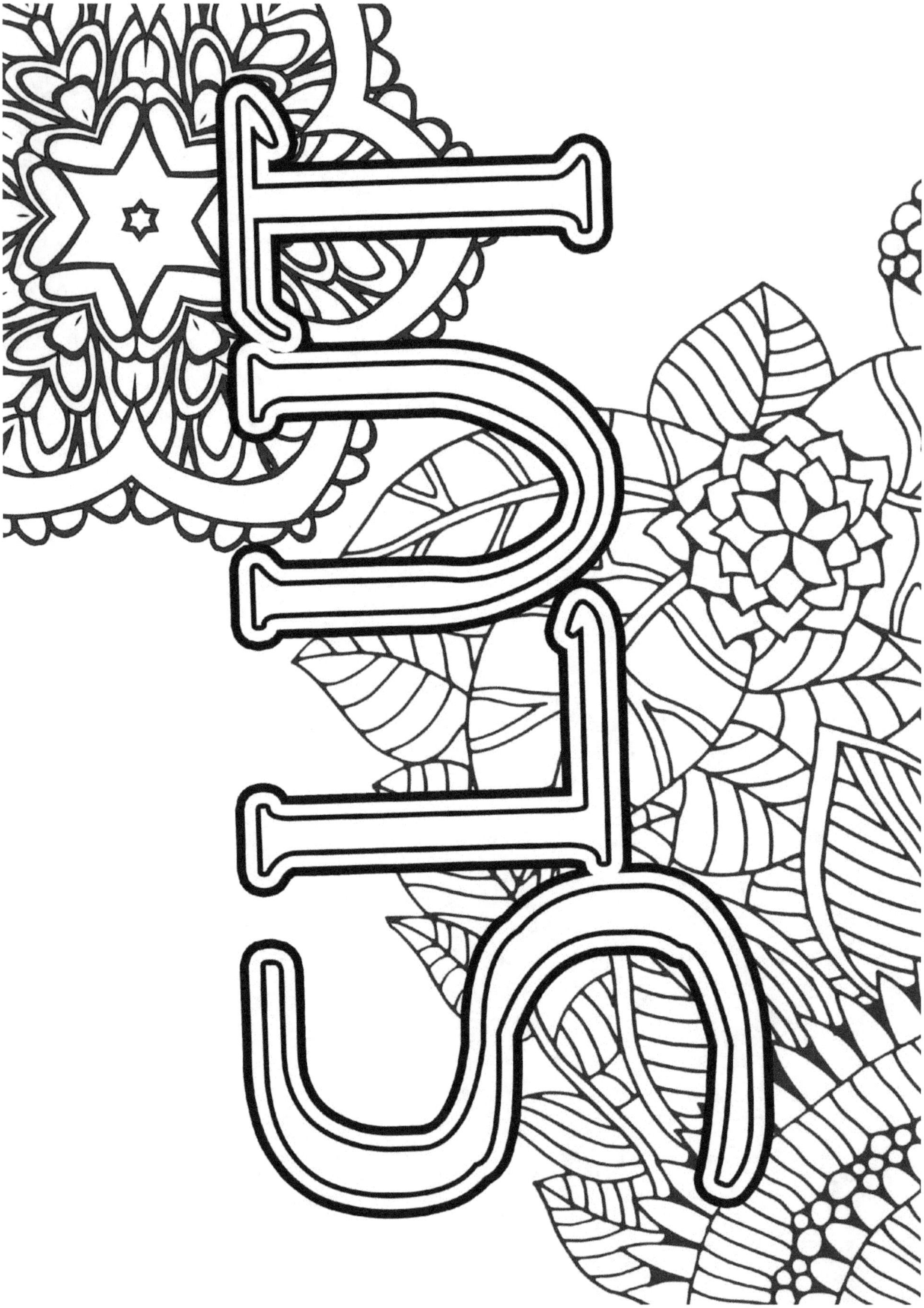
SLUT

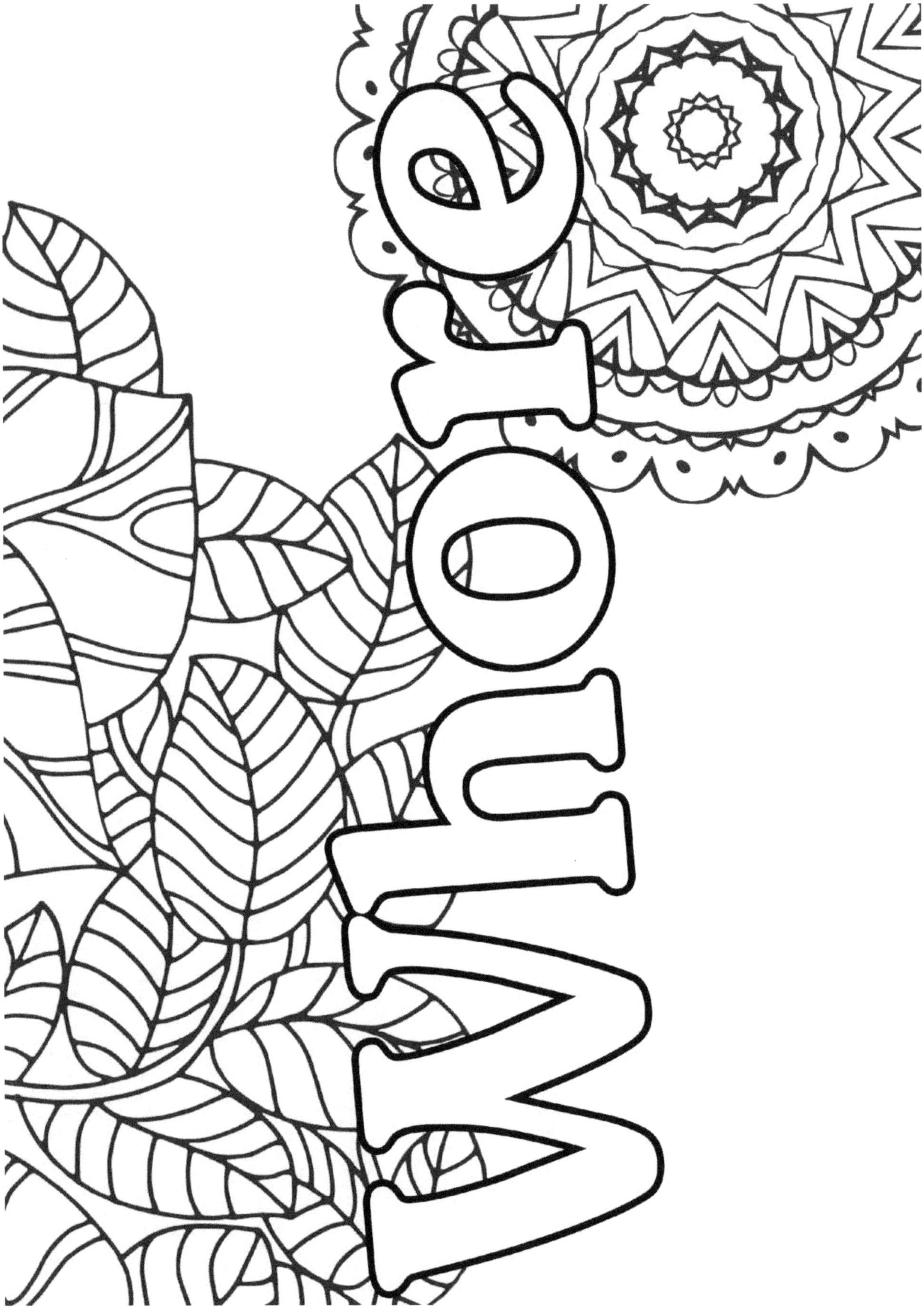
whore

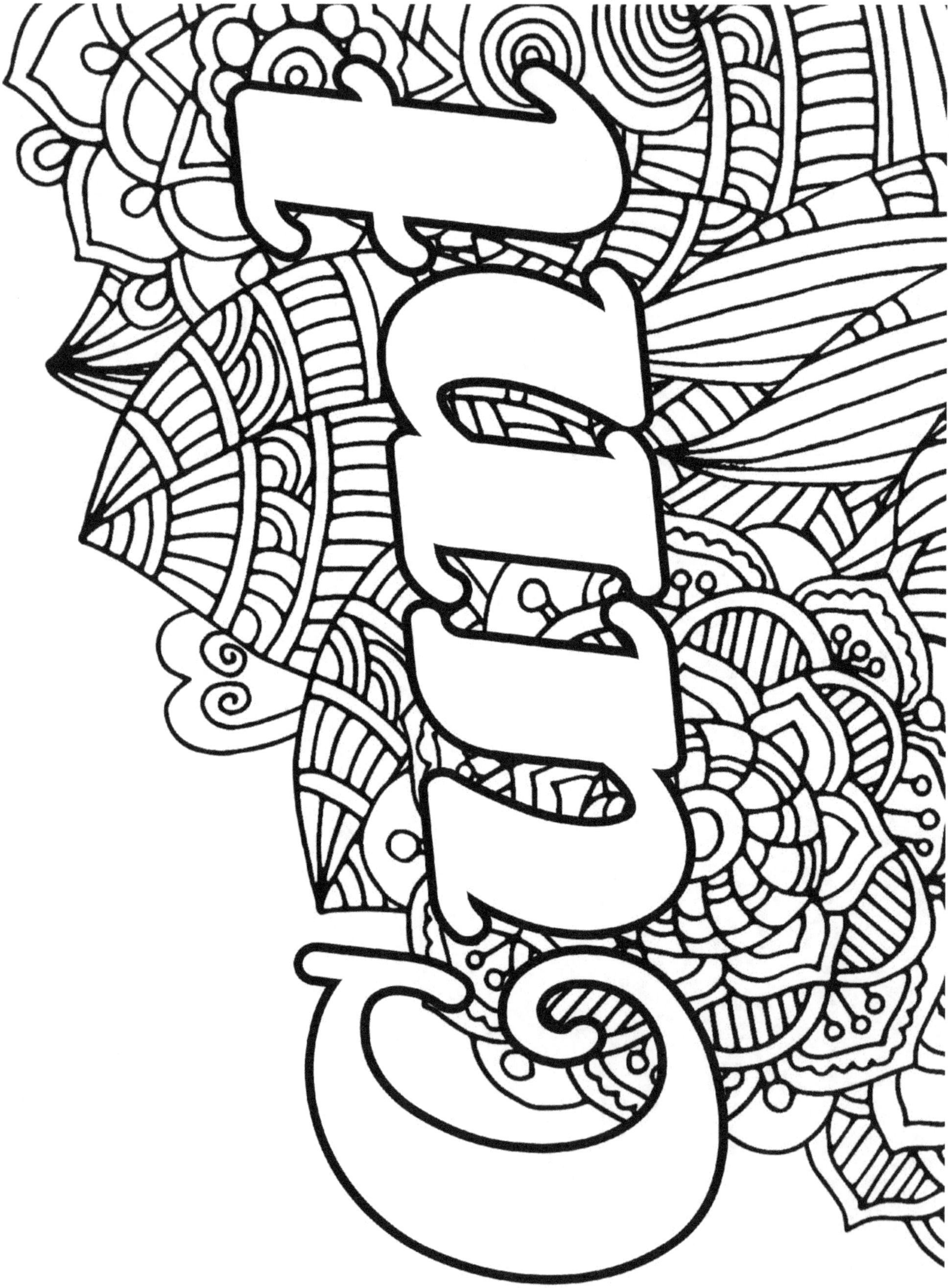
Cunt

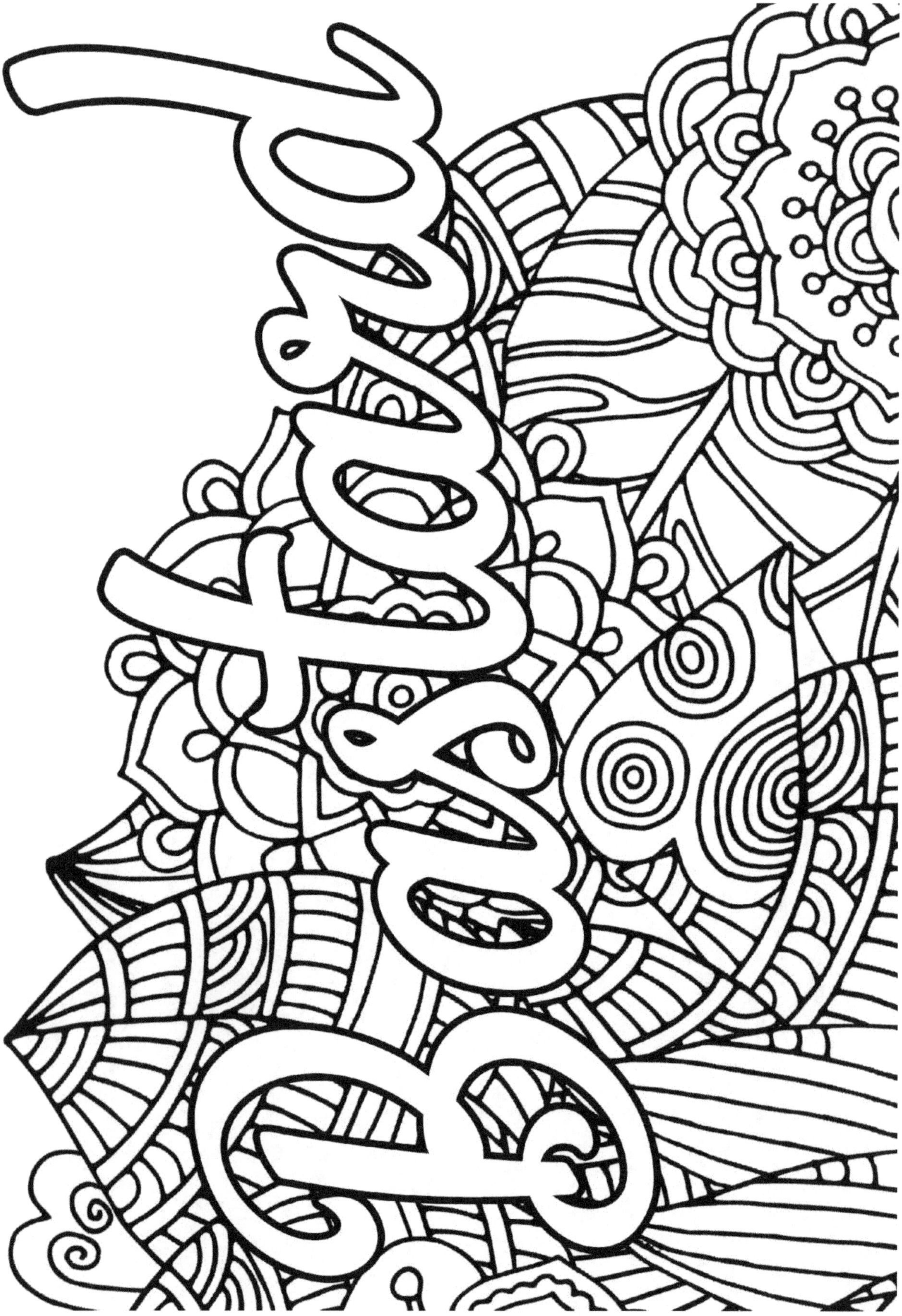
Bastard

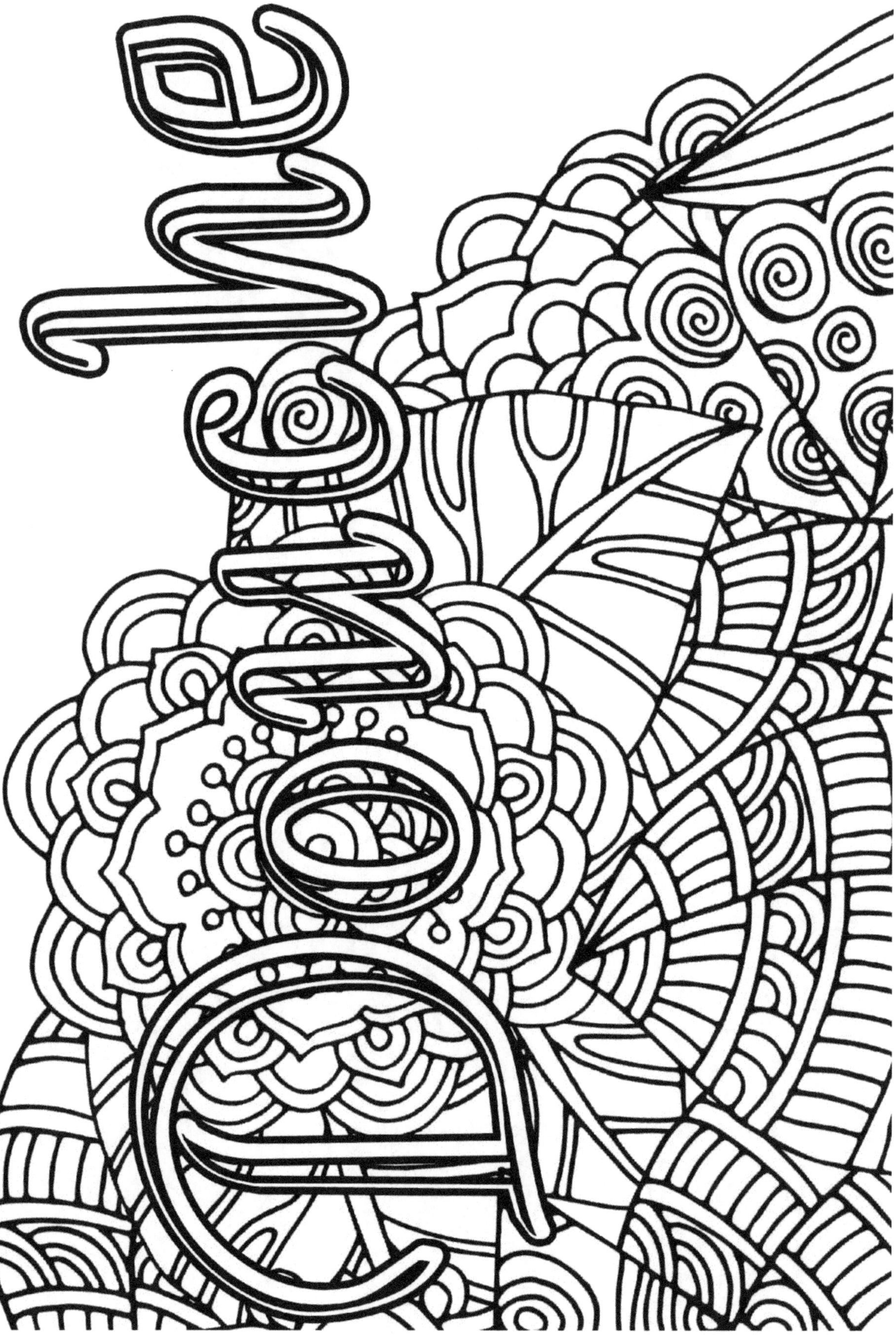
Douche

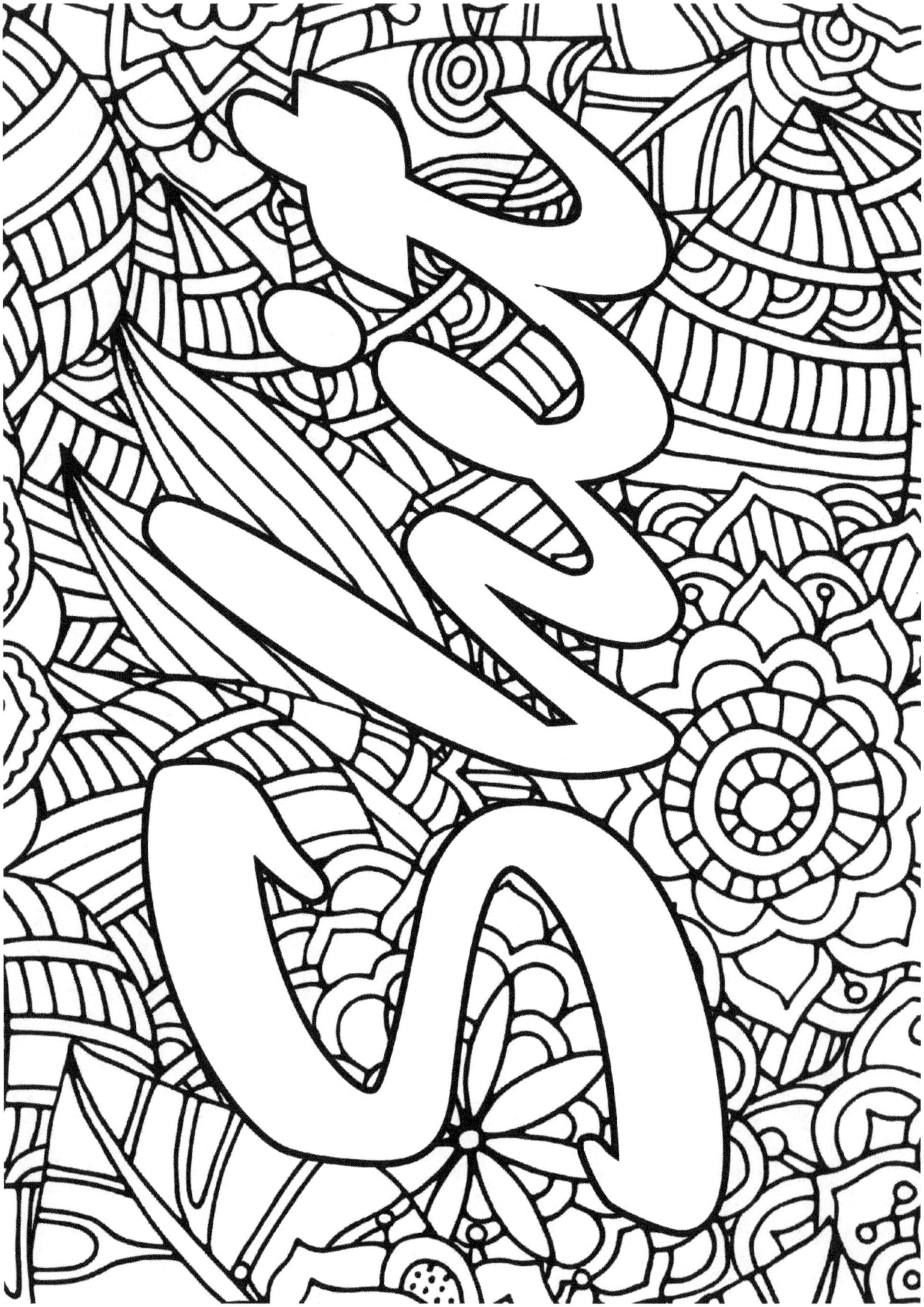
Shit

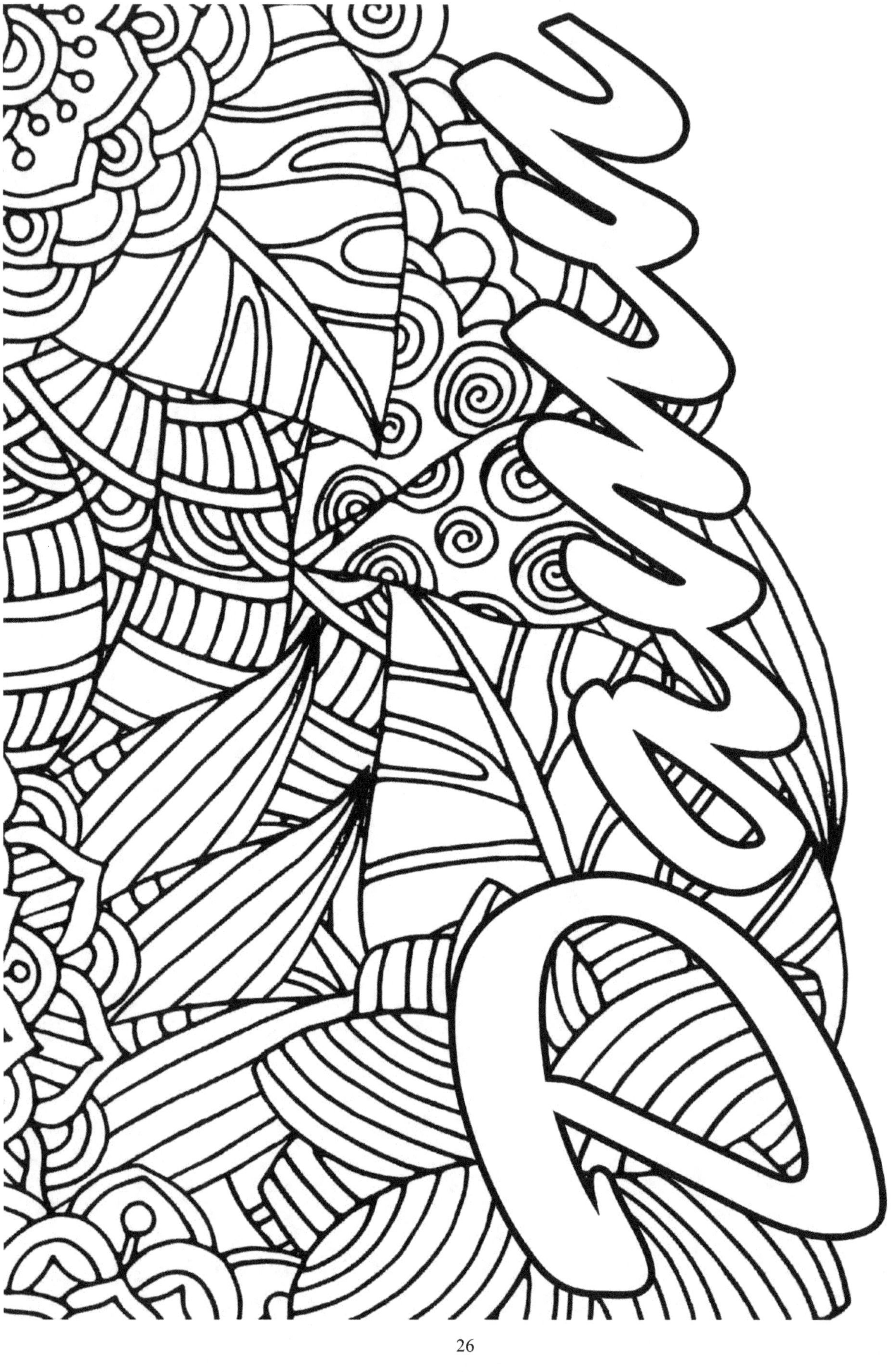

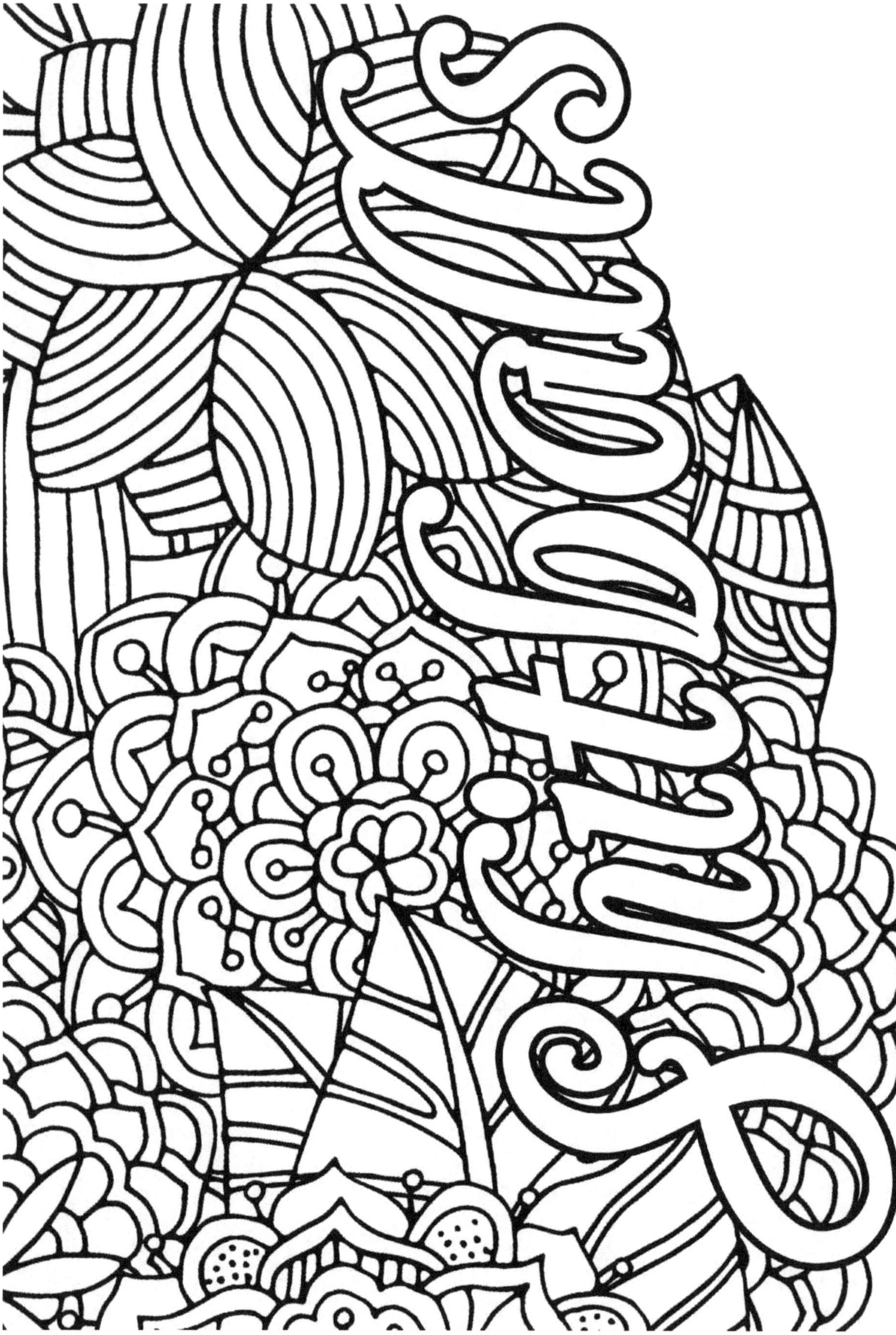
Shitballs

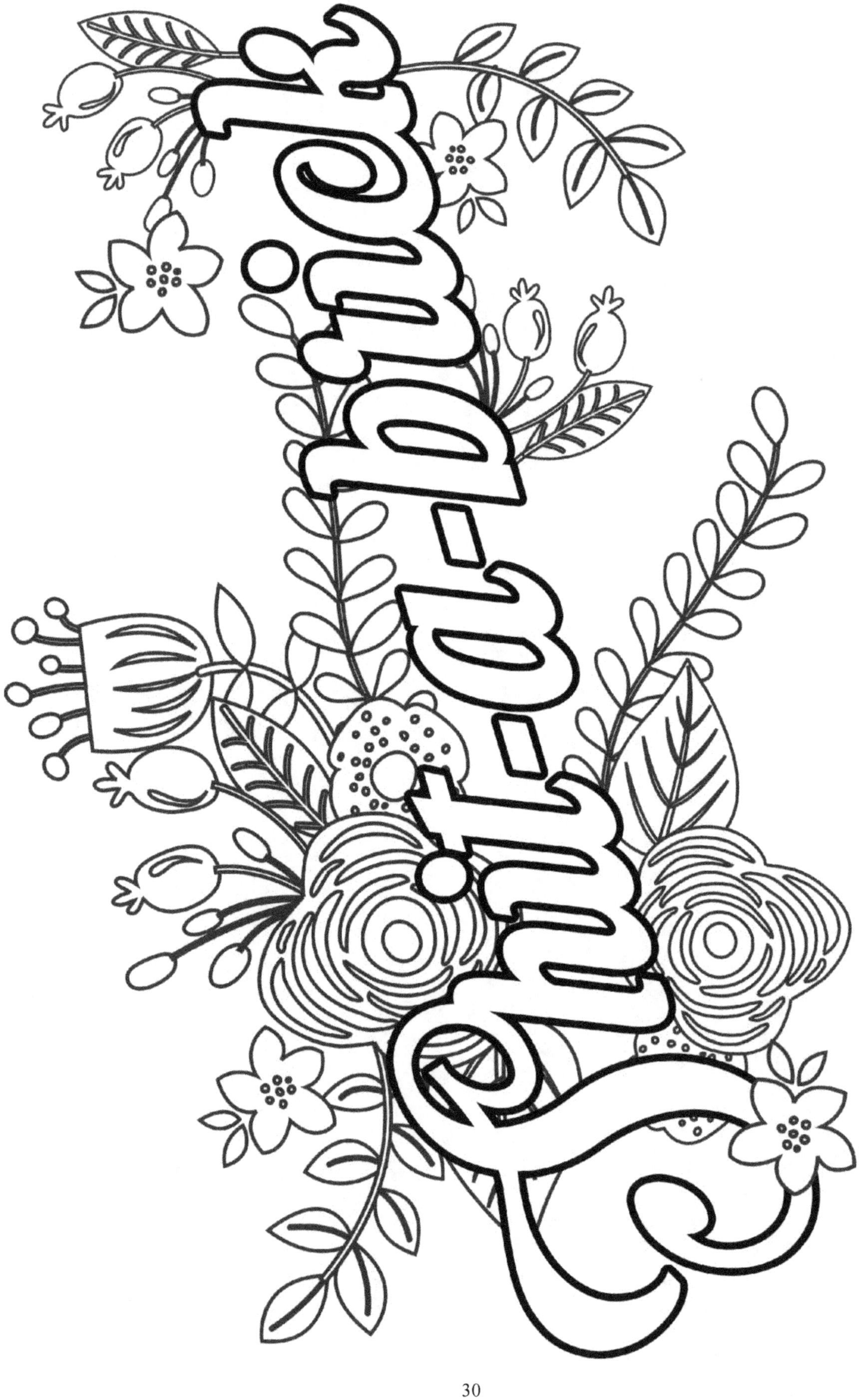
Shit-a-brick

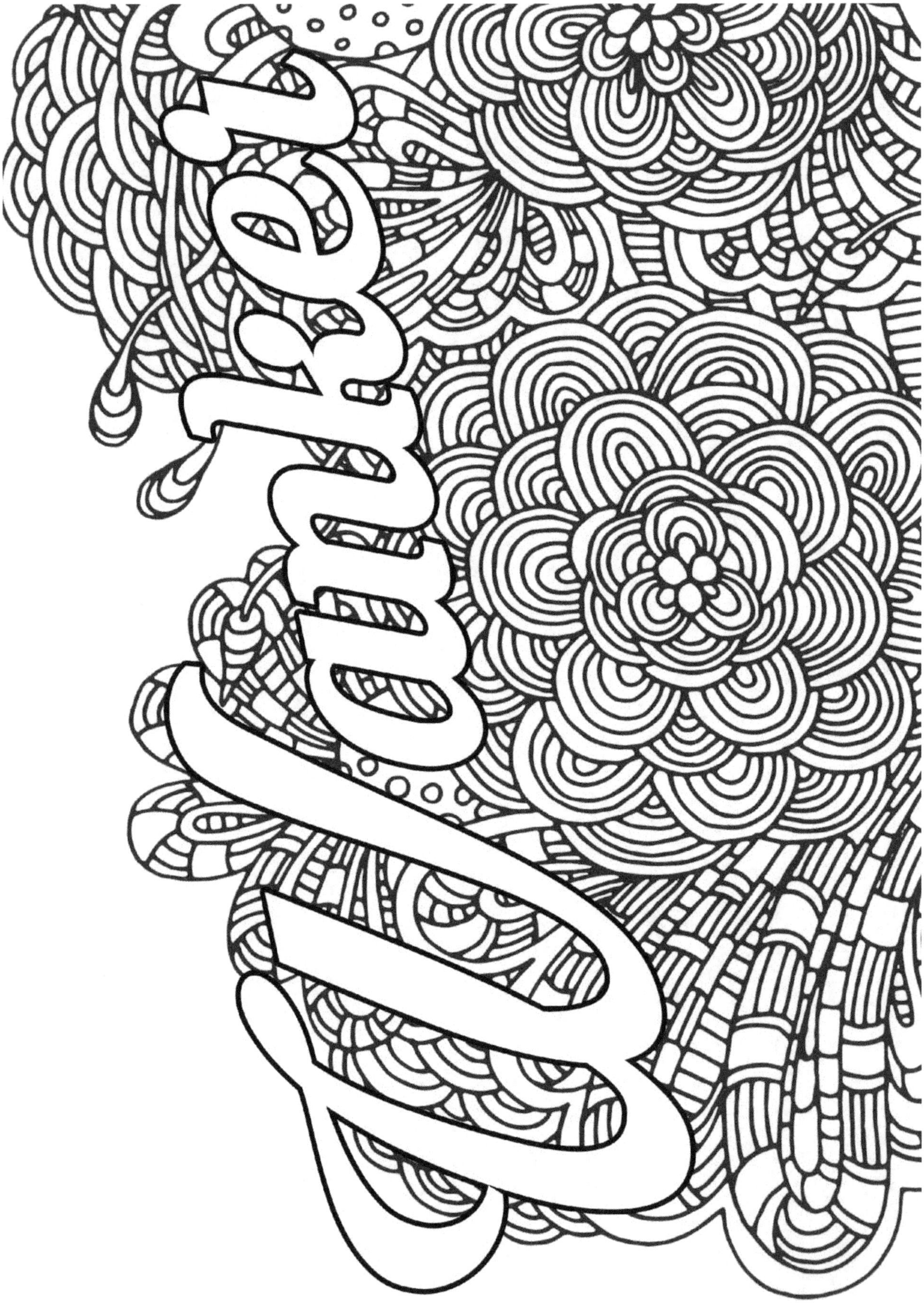
Wanker

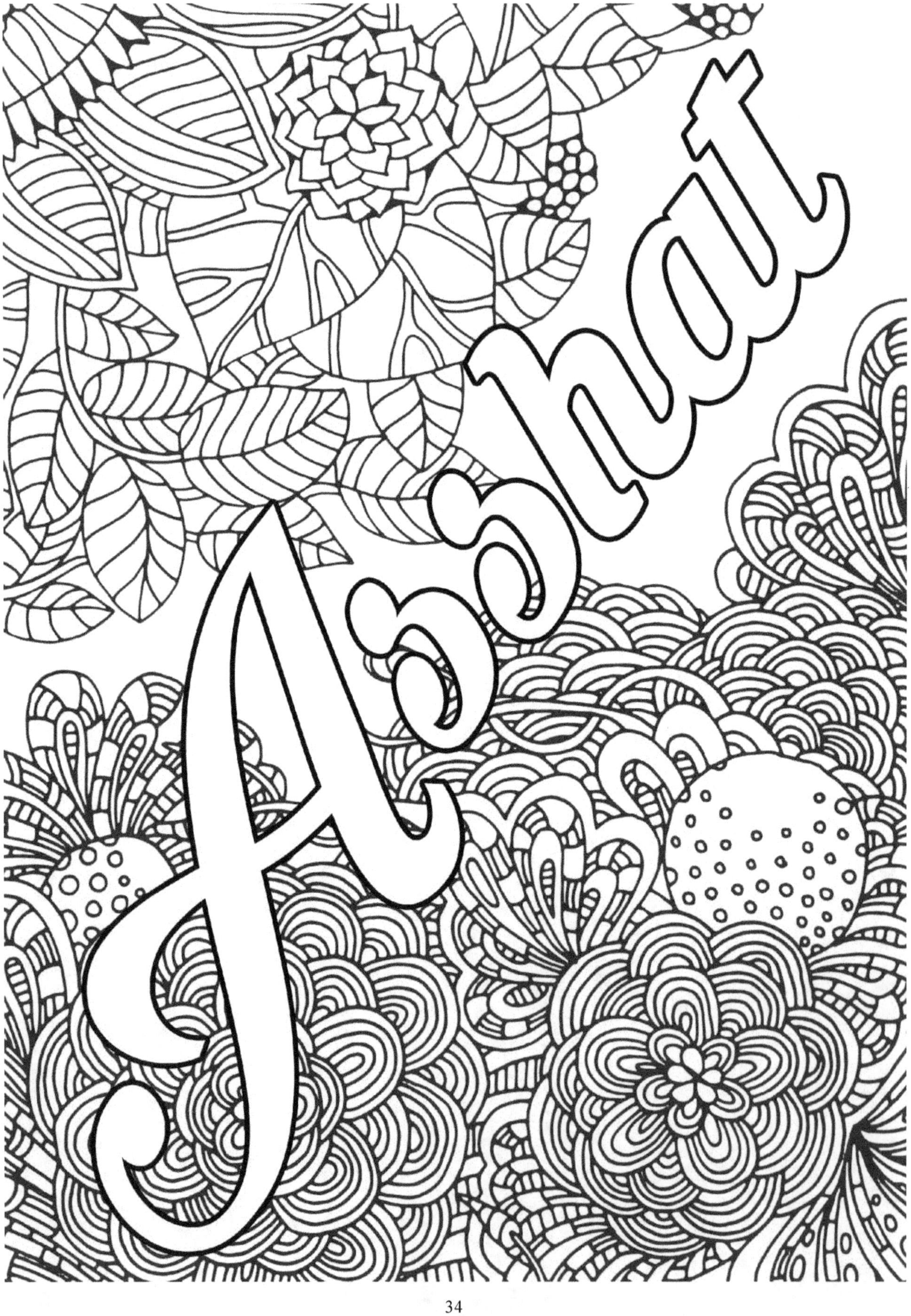
Asshat

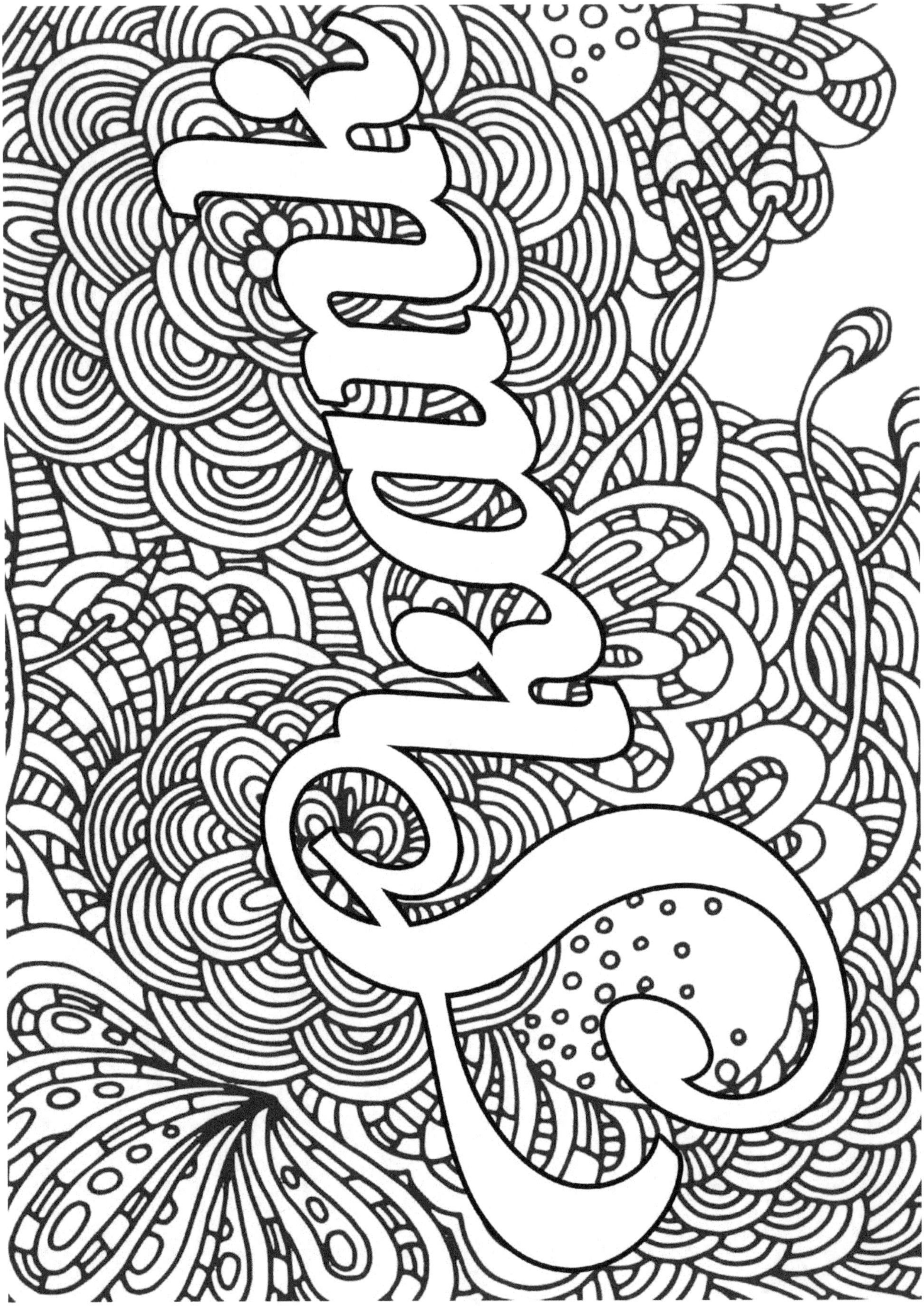
Seriously

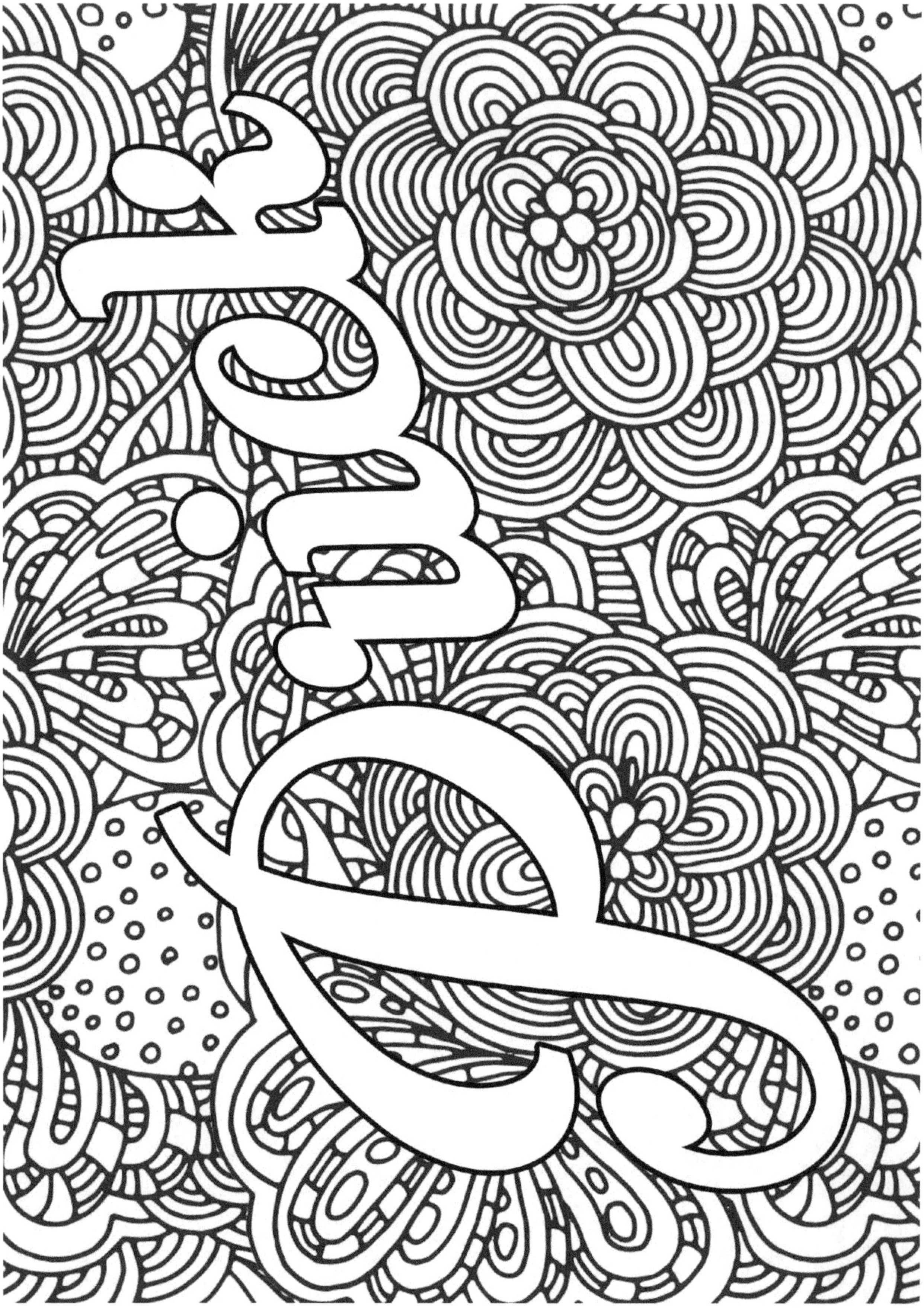
Prick

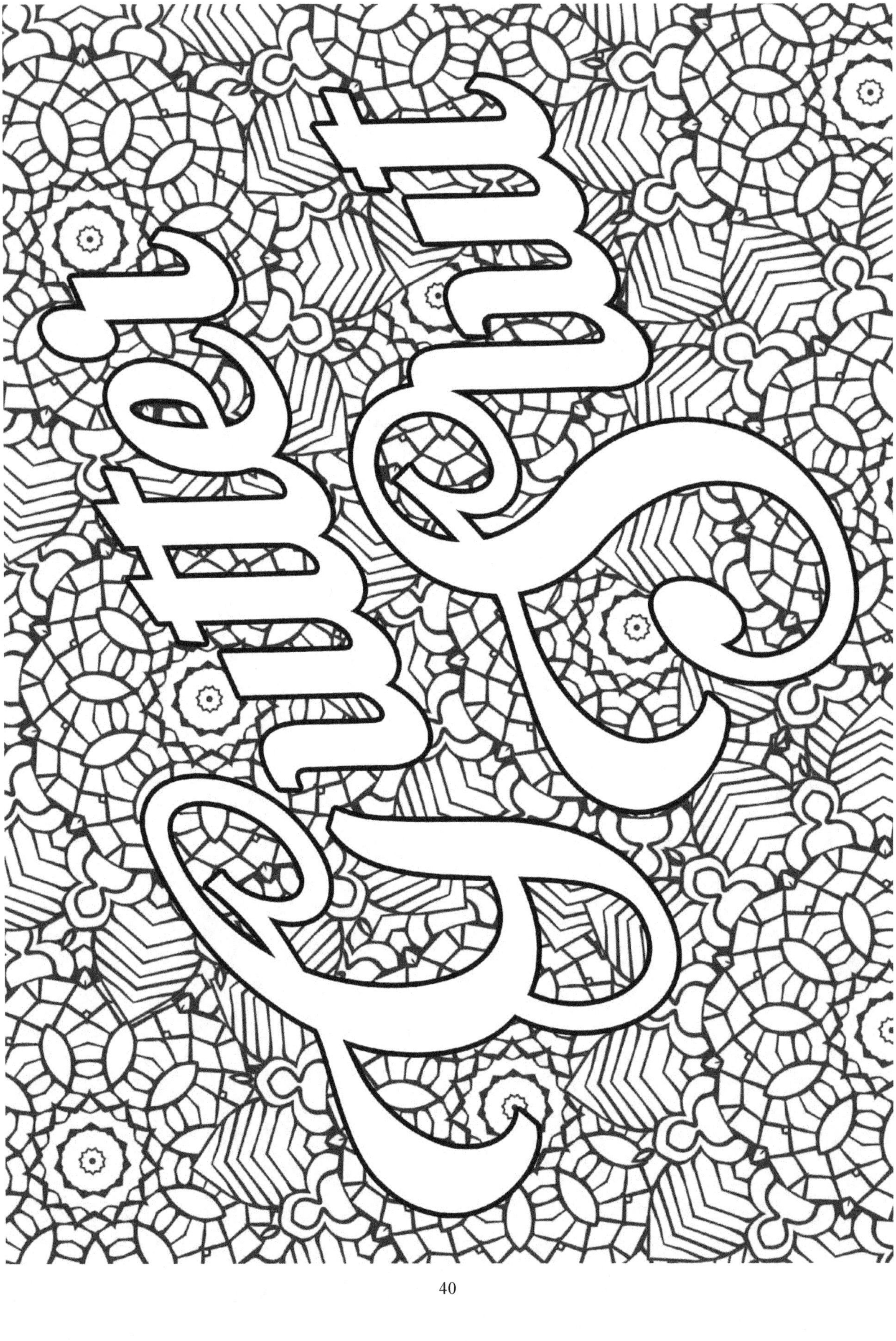
Gutter Slut

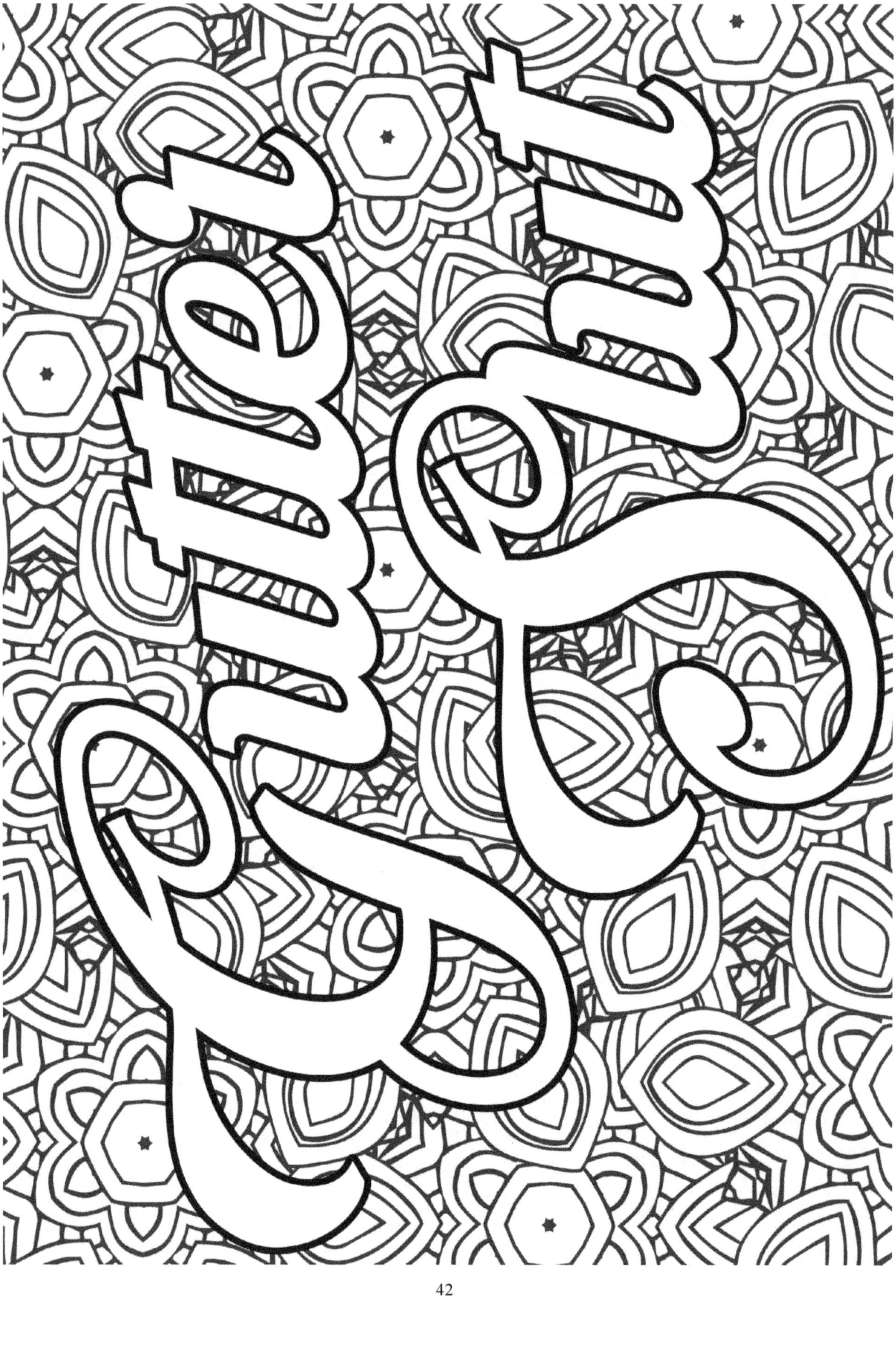
Gutter
Slut

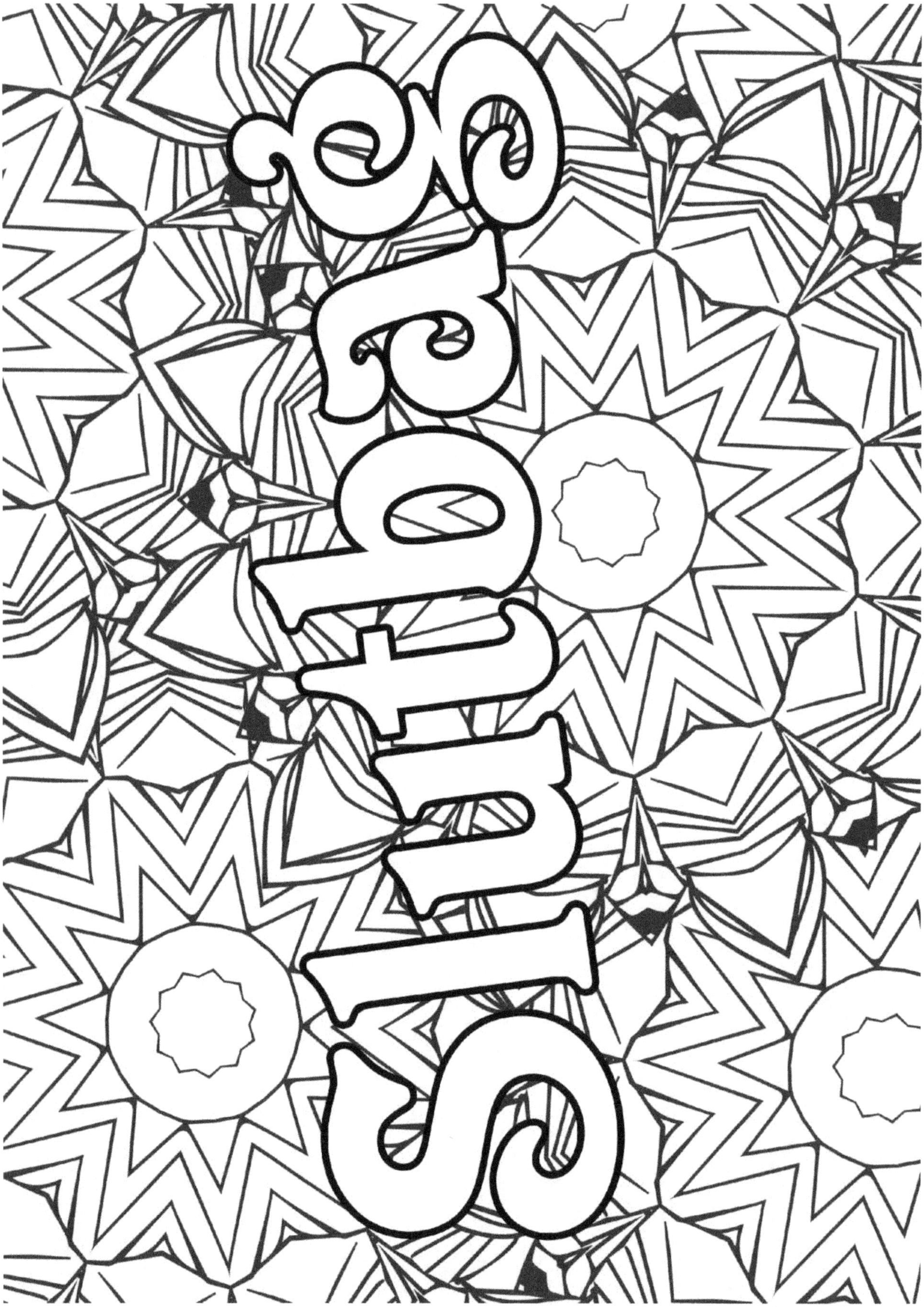
Slutbag

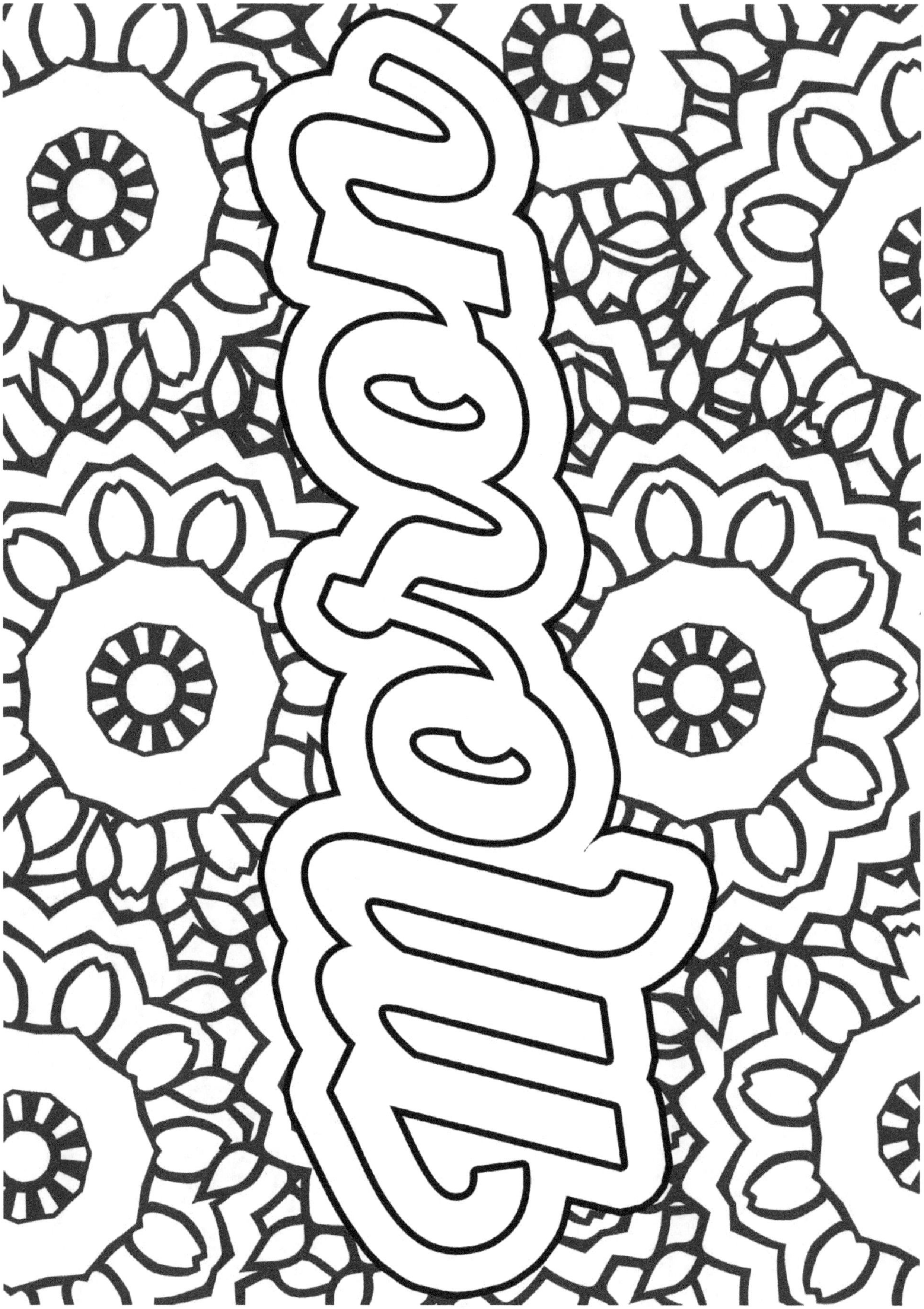
Moron

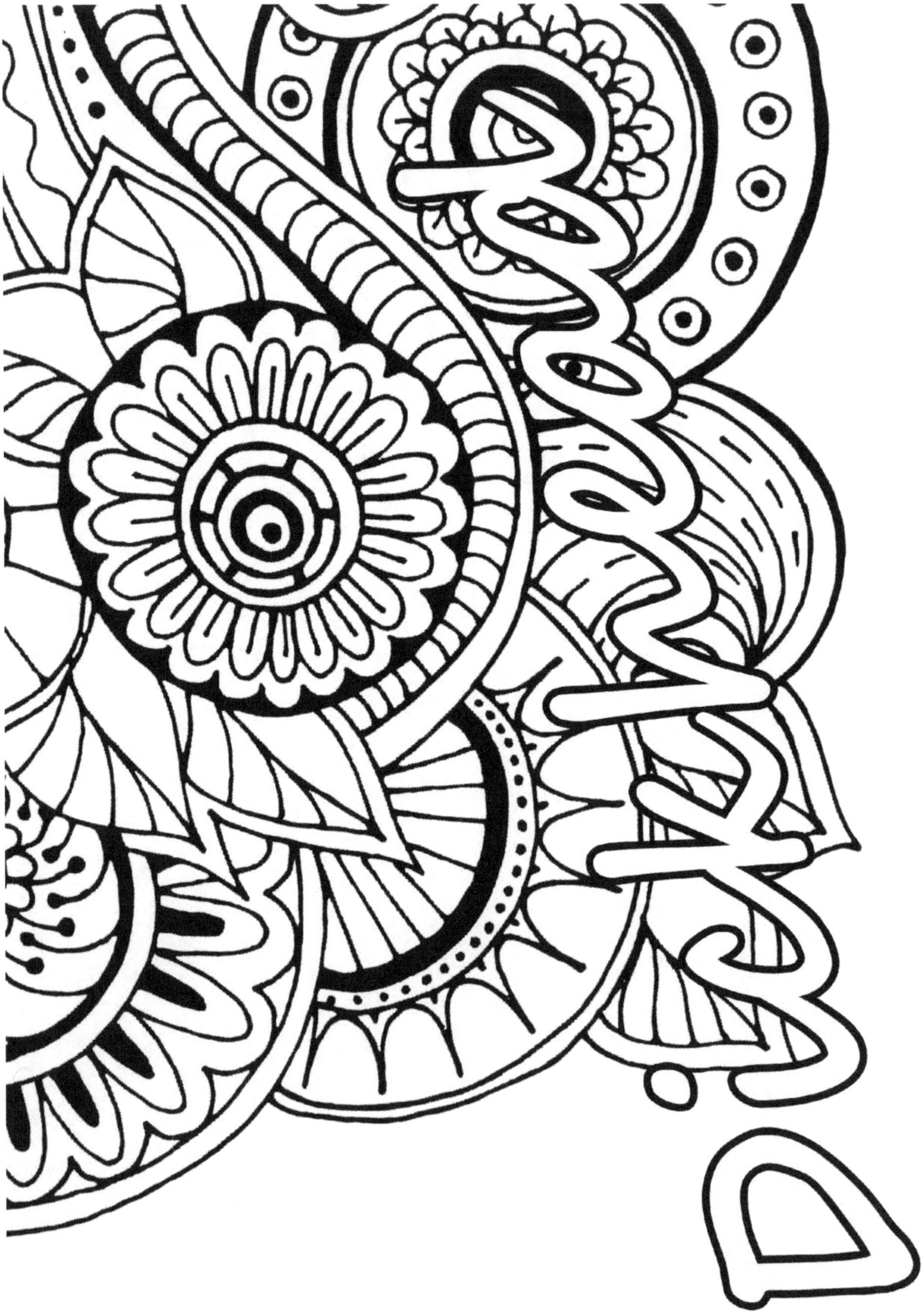
Dickhead

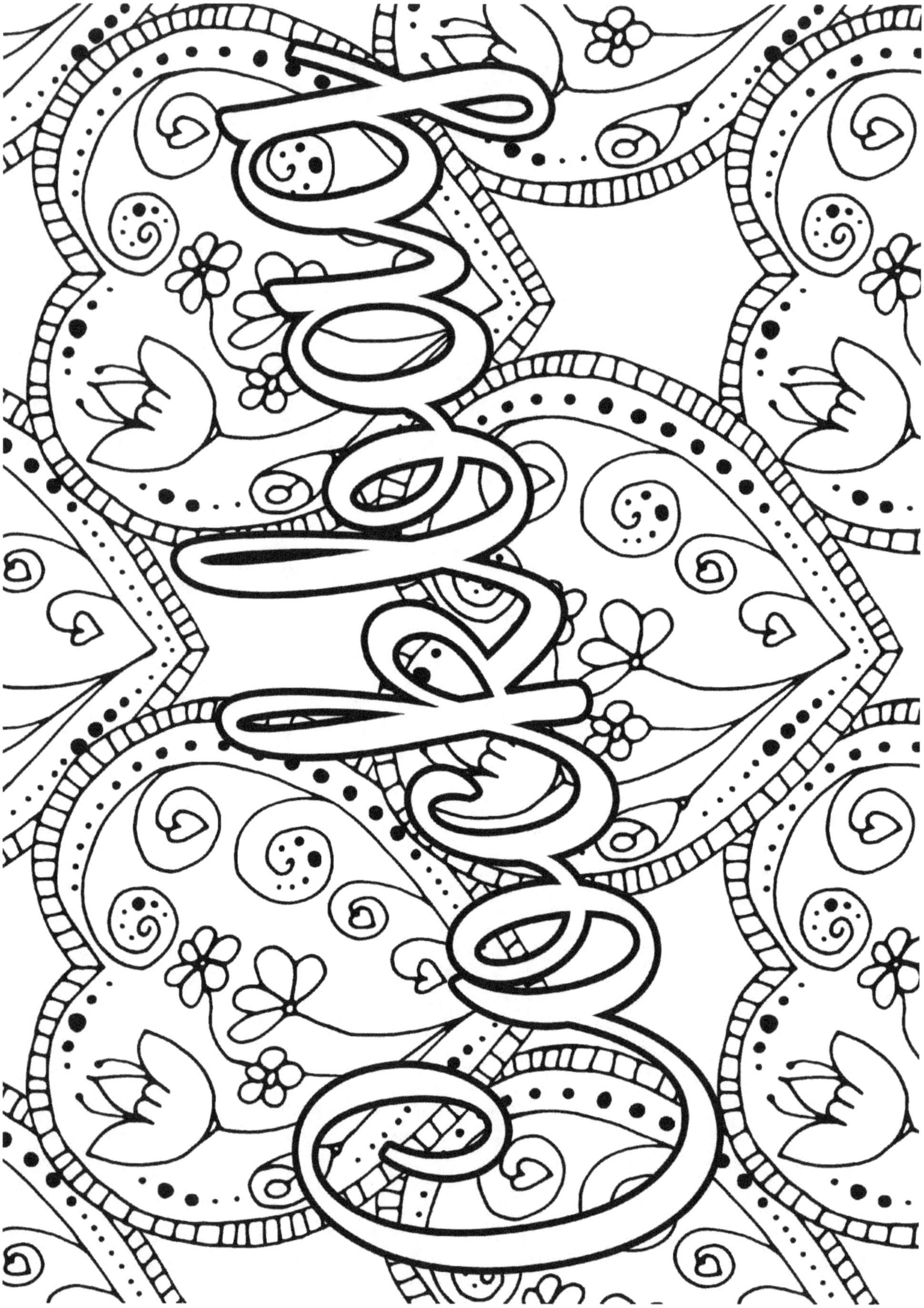
Cockbag

www.ingramcontent.com/pod-product-compliance
Lightning Source LLC
Chambersburg PA
CBHW080605190526
45169CB00007B/2881